Heading Out

Heading Out

Cosmic and Cryptic
Poetry and Prose

Roger Golden Brown

Golden Galaxy Publications

Published by Golden Galaxy Publications
Copyright 2015 Roger Golden Brown
978-0-9743513-0-8

All artwork was done by:
Robert Thompson and Brian Garvey

Please contact me if you have any questions.

I can be contacted at the following e-mail address:
wordsmith@goldengalaxies.net

Visit my personal website:
https://goldengalaxies.net/

And check out my world affairs oriented website:
https://goldengalaxies.net/Quasar/

This book is available for sale at:
http://books2read.com/headingout

See all of my books at my Author Page:
http://books2read.com/rogergoldenbrown

Thanks

I would like to extend thanks to Fred, Russ, Karin, and Edi, and all my other friends and lovers who supported me and allowed me my truest spirit - enabling my soul to give rise to these cosmic, crazy, and cryptic poems and prose.

Heading Out

.... these days we saw that we could go on forever to the past where we had left a part of ourselves. That notion had been long since waiting for our simple participation. Now that we had finally decided to cooperate we found a willing partner in our dream worlds. The turf was there and all we needed were the right maps.

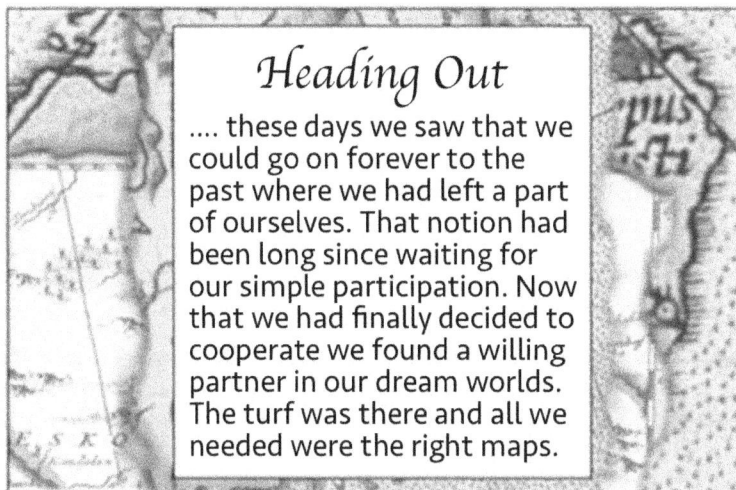

So grab aholt of the right maps
(or the best maps available)
and head out.

Read these poems for what they are. Words. Crafted together (I give myself too much credit) from all the words I know and some I don't know. Most of them just spilled out of me, needing just a little shaping to become something I liked (usually). I think they all mean something and say something, though I'm not sure. Read them, be sure you know what they are about.... or not. Agree, disagree, be challenged, be amused, be turned on. And hopefully enjoy. Maybe they will help you find your way home (if that's where you want to go).

In any case, stumble on sweetly.

Most of the poetry in Heading Out flowed out of my mind and pen during a prolific period of lyric writing in the 1980's and 90's. Later on in the 2000's I had a brief era where I wrote a handful of new poems and prose of a very different flavor; these perhaps a little looser. Finally I include a section of poemlets and writings dredged up from the way back.

The Peak Poetry Era

Apple Blessing

Apple blessing,
Thanks for the Fall,
I'm glad I'm here,
To heed the call.
I'd do it again,
And I'm sure I will.
I die by birth,
And to live I kill.
Say no to nothing.
And know true peace,
Live yes always.
And allow the release.
Day by day,
Time's to us beholden.
No beginning, no end,
We've always been golden!

Birdsong

Through the sheep dip
And the cow pies
Look for the Truth
Amidst the Lies.

Watch your step
As you wander alone
It can be slippery
And down you go.

That's alright
You'll be rebounding
You just fell
'Cause you needed grounding.

Through the sheep dip
And the cow pies
Seek out Freedom
And the where's and the wise.

You've set yourself up
You've let yourself down
Welcome to the club
You gorgeous clown.

Throw yourself a party
Come as you are
Naked as a jaybird
En route to the stars.

Through the sheep dip
And the cow pies
Don't ask the jaybird
Why it flies.

You must *feel* your way
Don't *think* you've gone wrong
All roads can be written
Into your song

So sing, my friend
The praises of flight
Sing them out loud
Like a clown outasight.

Sail your deep ship
Steer past the cow pies
Set your sextant tonight
To the center of the skies.

Breathe into your sails
Laugh at it all
Truth of it is
That birds never fall

Confidence is all
That it takes to master
The making of your way
Through the pasture.

Blind Nostalgia

Snow can waken
forgotten memories.
A child knows no cold
Knowing mama's meal will
Warm the freezing finger tips.

Wet dust in a sparse rain
Takes me back to
Corners of time locked away
On ancient playgrounds.

Was the snow really warmer?
There's no cold in a picture
But now I remember clearly
How numb were my lips.

It's been dry so long and
I have never lived
In the desert before;
What memory have I found.

Blind nostalgia brings
Bitter sweet longings
Unsure what turning
The key will release.

Wet leaves
Church bells
Flute birds

New mown grass
Crickets
Overheard words

Smell of hay
And a lazy
Summer airplane

Did it hurt;
That unseen snowball
Or was pain easier then,
Never being alone.

Curious echoes of
How simple it was.
Woolly summer seeds float
In it's only my mind.

Was the snow really warmer?
There's no cold in a picture
But now I remember clearly
I was chilled to the bone.

Summer was eternal for me.
It was someone else
Who carried on
When the sun ceased to shine

Blind nostalgia brings
Sweet and Sour longings
Unsure what turning
The key will release.

Blind nostalgia brings
Long lost longings.
Will the truth
Destroy the Peace?

Allowing Beautiful Creation
(Spring Fluff)

Always, always aching,
Building, breaking, baking,
Creating chilling chances,
Doing delicate dances,
Easily eating everything,
Foolishly freeing form.
Gilded gossamers glide,
Heavenly heathers hide,
In idle isolation,
Joining juicy jubilation,
Kissing-kissing-kissing,
Loving-Loving-Loving.
Mild meadow meads.
Nature's naked needs,
Overt occasions ooze,
Pause, ponder, peruse,
Quests quell quivers.
Rest's reassuring rivers.
Silky silence shuns,
Teasing teardrop tongues,
Unfinished, unplanned, unrehearsed,
Vast, vacillating, versed,
When we writhe
Xploring xquisite xtasies.
You'll yearn Yolanda,
Zenith-Zephyr-Zeal.

I am a Runnah

(be cool, man, read me beat)

I am a runnah.
From here to there
And from there to beyond
From now til forever
In my heart and my soul
I am a runnah.

I don't run miles
I don't run time trials
I dash and scamper
And don't let age hamper
My ability to fly free
I am a runnah.

(Up) Dash along the brick wall
(Down) And across the creek bed
Out the door (skip, dance, double step)
Stride off on my way
I am a runnah.

I'm in no hurry
I don't seek speed
Getting there faster (don't make no never mind)
I change directions in a flurry
I run on grass and weed
Slower or faster (don't make no never mind)

Cus .....
I am a runnah.

The Electric Indian

The Electric Indian
Could flow like the tides,
Then return to a square house
And listen to Lucy in the Sky.

The Electric Indian
Could feel the pulse of nature,
At night when the wires were still
And the organic machine would purr.

> Distant worlds occupying the same space
> come together through time.

Light is light,
No matter how it is made,
But the reach of the source
Affects every player in the game.

The Indian finds his power
Through currents never seen.
Broader and slower but not unlike those
That power his machines.

> To confuse the two is to forget who is
> the Brother and who is the Mother.

The Electric Indian has come once again
To the land of the land,
To try and ease the struggle
On this castle in the sand.

With this vision clear in his mind
He discovers much to his chagrin,
That he too must learn the lesson
That concentrated Power has forced on him.

> Which is to temper his self and look for
> answers in the mirror of the lake.

The Electric Indian
Yearns to live in total harmony,
But to be here in the jet age
Is simply his Karma, you see.

All through the sojourn
Many challenges arise;
It's so hard to know when and where
And how much to compromise.

> Communion demands that wires and
> willows sway side by side for a while.

The Electric Indian
Moves through Space and Time,
Seeking inexorably, magnetically
To heal and be healed by his own kind.

Spring's Sappy Release

Below the fleecy clouds
We while away the day
Amidst scattered sunshowers
Propelled by the juggernaut of time.

Were we to but see
The flowers, likewise ourselves
Pushing their way up
Richer would be the day.

Rivers swell with Spring's release
Emptying into a salty sea.
We swell also, seeking Spring's release
Being all of us, salty seamen.

Rabbits run and the first moth dies
Snakes bear young..... somehow.
Powerful eagles are born
As fuzzy humble gaping mouthed chicks.

When the first pea pods
When the first thistle bristles
When the sun is set free
Tis time to become gods again.

Yes, below the fleecy clouds
Harmony is a byproduct
Of attitudes sewn
In the winter's dismal drear.

Any sensible child of the universe
Feels the divine tendency
Towards holy indolence
And effervescent escapism.

Yes, Run, Rabbit Run
Lead the way
I'll follow fast as I can
Take me nowhere, and there I'll stay.

Under fleecing clouds
We while away the day
Innocent, dumb to the scheme
A part of it all.

Molecules to molecules
Sun rays to heaven
We are the axis
One with the wheel.

Of Life
Of Life
Ohhhh, ... Of Life

She's A Wild Beast

She's a wild beast.
She wants you for her feast.
Turn her on -
She'll prance and dance
And scream like a cat
And whinny like a horse.

She's a wild beast.
She wants you for her feast.
If you turn her on and
Give her half a chance
She'll lick you like a cat
And carry you like a horse.

She's a wild beast.
She'll have you for her feast.
Keep comin' on but
Relax your proud stance.
You've no need for that.
It's your body she wants of course.

She's a wild beast.
She's had you for her feast.
You turned her on and
You chanced her dance.
And she laid you on her welcome mat
And taught you there's beauty in force.

The Kitten and the Congressman

One moves spontaneously like a babbling brook.
One's actions must be affected to function with his colleagues.

One is naked, wearing only a fur coat bestowed upon it by God.
One wears a suit and tie in order to command respect.
  (It doesn't work, but he keeps doing it.)

One knows no limits, yet doesn't overstep its niche.
One, in doing his job, makes laws that say "no."

One only squeaks and purrs, yet we understand.
One's expressing himself is intently limited and focused.
  (Yet stifles communication.)

One can hardly be taught a thing.
One spends 1/3 of a lifetime being trained.

One you know is right because nature is right.
One you support because you believe yourself to be flawed.

One is somewhat wild.
One is somewhat civilized.

One doesn't care one iota about you and your welfare, and
  brings you joy.
One is dedicated to justice, and complicates and ties your life in
  knots.

One will grow up and be capable of eradicating rats.
One goes to Capitol Hill fearing the grace of cats.

Missing and Aching

Missing and aching will brew
A potent potion for Love.
But in their fulfilling
Does the potion pale?

Fear not. Nature has a cure;
Believe me, I've heard from above.
It's in the eyes of each other;
There exists no holier Grail.

(Be not afraid of the animal within.)

Moon and Tide People

We're not 9 to 5 people
We're moon and tide people
Be safe as popes, ankles and ropes
Or sleep in cloaks, under the oaks.

Popsicle Process

Popsicle process
brings freedom ... in heat.
What was ice
yields a watery treat.
When we allow ourselves
to have what we need
That water fertilizes
and brings life to our seed.

Oughta Have

Oughta have
What I gotta have
Don't be late
Or capitulate
Wisdom fares
Well within

Frustration

Nerves are swords, not at peace
you feel folded, against the crease
like the warp and woof of unsubstantial cloth
you won't hold together, as if eroded by moth
Oh the desire to express the heart
through the body freely flowing
their unused touch, the lovers apart
there's no release, the tension's growing
You could forget, but you don't want to
the longing's bad, but you need to know
your mate is out there, thinking of you
like a powder keg, you're ready to blow

Dead Wood

My talents are mute and moot
I need first to be needed
To be freed and seeded
I am dead wood turning to stone
My juices need to flow
And they need someplace to go.

Puzzle

While singing the praises of me, your name came up.
While singing the praises of you, I thought of myself.
Like my jigsaw puzzle with no edge pieces
I am at loss as to where to begin.

Everything seems to be fitting together
But I don't have the feeling it's moving.
Somehow I hunger for the satisfaction
Of completing the border, having the size of the game
    defined and filling it in.

If I'm up all night writing a poem
It seems worth it.
But my body complains, my throat is sore,
And the rules don't seem fair.

It's curious how things can seem clear at night
Even though it's hard to see.
But maybe that's just because the darkness of night is a
    great equalizer.
This puzzle came with no picture as a guide and now it
    doesn't seem to make much difference.

I know what it's supposed to be a picture of though
Because the box it came in had a title.
Still I wish I'd gotten it new
And been able to rip the cellophane off, secure that no one
    had lost any pieces.

Heading Out

When I got it, I laid it out flat on the table
And started by turning all the pieces right side up.
And with no picture as a guide
I looked for the most outstanding features.

What I found were two bright blue eyes
And I knew they were mine.
My gut told me they belong at the center.
But where exactly is the center of a puzzle with no edge?

I worked day and night on that puzzle;
I couldn't seem to let it go.
But sometimes when I was off having fun,
I'd come back and somebody had done some for me.

The face was mine; I knew that.
There were unmistakable qualities.
But sometimes, especially at night, I'd see you in it.
And marvel I'd never noticed the similarity before.

A day came when I was sure I would finish.
The ragged edge with no border pieces bugged me
But it was coming together and I felt smug
In a job well done, however odd a job it was.

As fate would have it, I was disturbed
By a knock at the door.
And out of the night, stepping into the light,
Came a new friend.

I welcomed her in,
Having been well trained as a host.
I explained I was busy working,
But almost done, come and see.

She smiled like she knew something I didn't.
I felt a sense of deja vu, but it passed.
There was a sense of thrill and foreboding in the air.
I wasn't sure if I felt strong or weak.

I went to my puzzle to show off my progress.
My new friend laughed
And it was an infectious laugh and I laughed too.
To this day I don't know why.

Out of her bag, she pulled a box
And handed it to me.
"A gift", she said.
It was another jigsaw puzzle.

Or should I say more jigsaw puzzle,
Because right away I saw a piece
That fit my unbordered edge
And I noticed yours had the same title as mine.

UnTruisms

Power corrupts
Or so they say.
I don't know;
Feel the Power
Of a roll in the hay.

Money is the root of all evil
It is thought.
That our roots
Could be so shallow
Seems to me quite odd.

An idle mind is the Devil's playground
Is the fear they instill.
This concept, generated
From a congested head
Fears the freedom to kill.

Aquarius

Pack away your fears
For the next 2,000 years
Feel the world changing
Look at the Earth, it is green
What used to be so transparent
More hidden Truths now are seen
Each and every Truth, all seen in fun
Now a tribe of Truths becomes One
I am an Aquarius
I am a Captain of Light

Miramanee

You never come across the stream to see me.
And while I wait so patiently,
Each night I watch the shadows on your teepee.
I love you and I know you'd love me,
    if you'd only meet me.

By day I carry water and cultivate corn.
At night I study Kant, Hegel, and Spinoza till dawn.
I'm wise, intelligent, and loving.
I'm wise, intelligent, and lonely.

Why don't you come across the stream and see me.

I've written you messages, on my best papyrus.
Letters of love, suggesting a tryst.
But my eagle refuses to deliver them.
He says you don't even know I exist.

The stars will spin for us; I know it.
I've watched you pick flowers; your body shows it.
In your face I see such Peace; won't you share it.
I'm so crazy for you; I just can't bear it.

I think I'll carve a totem, full of symbols,
Tall and straight as night.
When I see you bathing in the stream,
I'll bring it down, so polite.

While the water runs off your breasts
My heart will skip a beat.
I'll sit cross legged across from you
And pray for world peace.

Maybe then you'll feel me;
Feel the love in my soul.
Naked, you'll wade across the stream,
And eat berries from my wooden bowl.

We'll share our dreams for the Giant Family,
Under Brother Sun above.
Then we'll act completely selfishly,
And just for us, under Sister Moon, we'll make love.

Saturnfaction

You wore Saturn's rings
among other things
(the way it wanted to go)
made you so hard to hold
But my heart always sings
No, traveling out of its reality
Frees me to my frailty
Rapidly, as it seems to me
As it floated on its rusty wings
Iron feathers falling loudly through the clouds
Down, down, down - Quenched peace ripping
    radical shee-bop.

- Saturnfaction was created by 5 of us seated in Saturn Cafe in Santa Cruz one evening. Myself, Ken Ohm and 3 others taking turns writing lines. I wrote several of the lines and the final line, a tribute to the Beat era.

Call Me a Dreamer

Call me a dreamer
Call me a fool
I'll be the master
Why be the tool?
The work is Life
Each piece a jewel
You can take it or leave it
Believe it or not
So be taken and left
Or rewrite the plot
You're the one, not me
I'm the one, not you
To do to you to do me too.

Uselessness

I seek uselessness
Uselessness separates Fun from Work
It separates Being from Doing
And, alas, Peace and Goodness from War.

Hypnosis, Drip Noses

Tweedle Dee Dee, Tweedle Dee Dum,
Pick your nose with your thumb.
Paint a picture with your toe,
There are no rules which way to go.
When I say no, ignore it please,
Don't cover your mouth when you sneeze.
You can be as weird as you like,
You can even be black, instead of white.
I don't care, 'cause I am not,
Hypnotized; or bound with thought.

Tweedle Dee Dee, Tweedle Dee Dum,
Park Avenue or a slum.
You think you're different; you're really cool,
Doesn't matter which, if you follow a rule.
You act like you're supposed to,
I think you're like mosta you.
Don't ever ask why there's pie in the sky,
Or the grass is greener, when you know it's a lie.
You feel safe as a bug in a rug,
Hypnotized; it's better than a drug.

Tweedle Dee Dum, Tweedle Dee Dee,
You can change it, you see.
Feel your feel, it's what you are,
That's how you get to be a star.
Act your act and play your play,
You see, you're beautiful that way.
Love your Love and I'll love mine,
Really free, you can't help but shine.
You have a choice, so please be bold,
Hypnosis, drip noses. Shake the society cold.

Common Reality?

It's becoming quite apparent,
That I'm becoming more transparent.
On what I create, you can bet,
That what you see is what you get.

And yet,
Beyond your frame of reference,
You misunderstand the essence,
Of how I leap and fly,
So that my truth, to you, seems a lie.

But why?,
Ought not truth for one be truth for all,
Winter, Spring, Summer, and Fall?
It depends on whether you can simply be,
And get beyond your self made movie.

You see,
Until you bring the reels to a stop,
And your houselights all go up,
You'll keep expecting my life to fit,
And make sense with all your shit.

To which,
I must honestly confess:
We all got us all, into this mess.
And our plots are so thick you want to shout,
"I don't think we'll ever climb out!"

No doubt,
A common reality is a subtle inflection,
But I see steps in the right direction.
Pull the plug and walk outside;
Kinda scary, but trust me, you will abide.

So try,
To refuse to take on other's blame,
As you speak your truth, unashamed.
Tell the actor it's time to heal,
And acknowledge whatever it is you feel.

(now that's real)

Just Plain Love

So....., you put hope in the pope.
And you're still at the end of your rope.
You thought it would be so ecstatic.
What a dope.

I think it's time you got some rope,
Climb up to your own balcony and elope.
Clean all idol cobwebs from your attic,
Marry yourself and exile the misanthrope.

The pope is tucked neatly away in Rome,
Buddha and Christ frozen in some tome.
The interpretations are so erratic,
You'll find the answer in your own dome.

Look high or muck about in the loam,
You needn't ever leave your home.
"But, Oh God!, the answers are so enigmatic."
Not really. To Confucian, just say shalom.

"Praise Allah, I'm off on my pilgrimage.
I'll be ready soon; just gotta pack some baggage."
You're really not listening, so I'll be more emphatic;
See that tree? The highest truth is in its foliage.

Believe you me, you are that wise old sage;
Read any book, doesn't matter, turn any page.
When you forget what you're looking for, you'll be elastic;
Just plain love is the highest message.

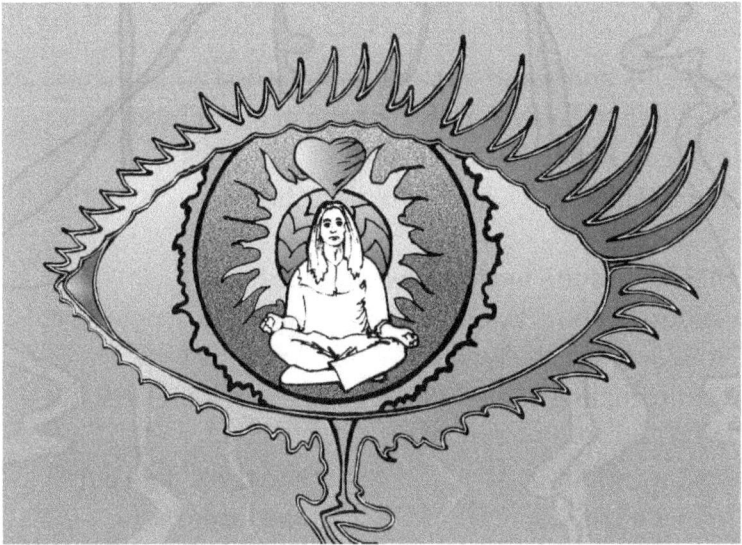

Needs and Time

Time, as we all know, is free.
So why treat it as an enemy?
What confuses the matter, truth is,
Are our needs when in a body.

Innocent, and naked as babes in the wood,
We come to earth, now feeling the need for food.
In the dark chamber we float,
Nature kindly providing for us as it should.

Then comes the time to leave the cozy nest,
Pandora's box, now open, reveals earth's treasure chest.
From our long soul's night we now know day.
Our fluctuating bodies' needs compel us to the breast.

Time works for us all   Time takes time out
Time is a crime   Time races on
Time is sublime   Time's so long

Time fits like a glove
And the time is right
If you take time with love

Certain freedoms lost, we take on responsibility.
But given half a chance, we naturally forage from the
   cherry tree.
When night comes, with its companion cold,
We can, as community, shelter ourselves quite happily.

Naked we come, the rhythm of breath is heaven sent.
But we're taught to work; time put in is money spent.
People who play the game, the lords of the land,
Foist upon us their paradigm, demanding the hell of rent.

It gets so complicated, easy to lose the flow.
In competition, we're numb to what we feel; we forget
   what we know.
But with Faith in action, time is friendly to our needs.
Our harvest is fruitful; truly, what we reap is what we sow.

Time works for us all   Time takes time out
Time is a crime   Time races on
Time is sublime   Time's so long

Time fits like a glove
And the time is right
If you take time in love

Time fits like a glove
And the time is right
If you take time with love

New Age Cretins

Banish all New Age Cretins
Replace them with primitive savants
Bring on a new day (like always).
Full of ignorant Wonder

Leave the new age on its pedestal
Of smug rhetoric
While life takes place
On solid ground

Did your workshop cost enough to be valuable?
You learned why you've had problems in the past
And in an open hearted loving supportive environment
You learned new skills.. which will get you through next
    Monday

You've freed the child within
But do you care at all
To re-raise that brat
Without all the baggage this time?

Abundance is the cornerstone of your philosophy
More of everything everybody wants for just chanting:
"I deserve it. Listen up Universe.
Me, me, me."

A little louder now.
With a little more faith now
Yes, I hear the presses. They're making more money in
    case it catches on and we all deserve it
Yes, I feel the earth super charging with more raw
    materials for Me.

So banish all New Age Cretins
Hang them upside down from their gravity boots
Until they spill their guts
Fertilizing the Earth for real growth

Full of ignorant Wonder.

Peas in a Pod

We're all peas in a pod,
You 'n I 'n God,
But why distinguish?
Instead of constant service to the cult of personality,
Just let go to a finer reality,
There's nothing to relinquish.

Some think our paths unique,
So much to misunderstand and critique,
You love it, thinking it's life's mystery.
True, we all have our own mode,
But we'd all be on the same road,
If liberated, free of history.

Protecting our past, insisting on our own pain,
Taking so much attention to maintain,
Wallowing in the darkness of stagnation.
Peas in a pod is right
At home, in the present, in the light,
If freed of the illusion of separation.

Ohne Kaffee

Ohne Kaffee, wie wirst du munter in der Früh?
Das Sehnen nach dem Duft der Blumen im Garten?
Der Pfad des Schmetterlings durch die Strahlen der
    Morgensonne?
Die Verlockung des Sommerteichs mit Schilf rundherum?
Oder der zu erwartende Schweiß von Sex oder Sport auf
    der Wiese?
Ich weiß nicht.

Perilous Pleads

Perilous pleads
bring beautiful
beads

Of sweat
on the forehead
of time

Bellingham's Georgia Pacific

It is, in deed, horrific,
You rape the word pacific,
To be more specific
You're Georgia Putrific.

It's not much to ask
To have fresh air to breathe
But I feel like I've been GiPd
Every time my house I leave.

24 hours a day you drone and crash;
Gotta keep pulling in the cash.
The forests dwindle,
Now horizontal in your yard.

What used to be shoreline
Has now no soul or heart.
Sure you think there's no other way;
Got workers in this county gotta get paid.

If you cared to learn,
You'd find the fibers from grass
Make a better friendlier paper,
With which to wipe your ass.

But what's a person to do
About your stench?
I'm at a loss.
In this town you're so entrenched.

I guess your smut
I'll just leave.
And wipe my butt
With a leaf.

And so to Bellingham's GP
I call you rather PU.
I've gotta breathe free.
And so, Adieu.

Lost and Found

In the forest lurk the elves.
Keep an eye out.
In the forest, it's dark and damp.
And kinda creepy.
    But don't worry.
In the forest, reigns perfect chance.
You might find some roots.
In the forest, there's springs and falls.
It's really dangerous.
    But don't worry.

(Because death in the forest is better
        than life on the streets)

Deep in the forest, time flows still.
You can feel that.
Deep in the forest, it's hot and cool.
Quiet sounds loud.
    But don't worry.
On the mountainsides, or in the vales...
My God, there's a snake!
In the trees, or floating in the air...
What was that?!
    Just don't worry.

(Because there's no way out... you're surrounded)

Everywhere in the forest, there's decay.
Look close, it's alive!
Everywhere in the forest looks new.
It's old as the hills.
    So don't hurry.
All over in the forest, life is tangled.
Listen to its order.
All over in the forest, it's sweet and flower.
You can smell your past.
    So don't worry.

(Because now you're really lost... you're almost home)

Tirol, 1993

I feel humbled and subdued.
What shoulda been sweet choir became the blues.
Let me tell you a tale of a long summer
And how I came to start wearing shoes.

I wanted to be slow, to live life slower.
I wanted life to flow, to live like a flower.
Packing in the Seeds of Change,
I returned to my roots to rearrange my suits,
Feeling alive and full of power.

I caught a plane, a bargain, it seemed
Through the blue, soft as silk, to the Alps.
With almost no dough,
But looking forward to some good bread,
Knowing my friends would try and help.

Had a place, I thought, for the summer to stay.
Turned out the house was already filled.
A family of fugitives from a You Go War.
Who, I guess, didn't want to be killed.
I could only stay a month; not much more.

With my computer along, I had my work.
I'd typed 8 months and with one to go,
I worked away, rain or shine, night and day,
Not realizing some of the nicest weather I'd blow.

Edi and small town Imst had been my goal
But Karin's city life social scene was attractive.
Imst was a small town gone bananas
And Innsbruck was a cold city hyperactive.

There's always a lesson to be learned,
Or so I've always thought.
When it felt like I'd been burned,
I sought the lesson I'd been taught.

I've been rollin' along and growin',
And seeking my ideals.
Life's been telling me and showin',
What feels the most real.

I want peace on our mother earth,
But there's just too much pain.
So me and King Arthur 'll have to wait
'Till it comes around again.

(And you know what I learned?)

I found that if you're gonna trip by flying,
You gotta look inside your mind.
And in bad weather, you just keep trying.
'Cause sometimes, you gotta fly blind.

Later Era Writings

Three Critters

Paradox

Now we all know how nice it is to know something for sure. No doubts. No ifs, ands, or buts. You're studying, you're reading, you're talking with a friend or taking a test. Or maybe more importantly you are debating. You make a point and you feel good. That's solid. Then.. wham. You get a Paradox thrown back at you.

The Paradox shatters your world. The Paradox jumps out, gets right in your face and says, "yeah, what you know is true, but the opposite is also true", messing with your head. How can that be? And yet, there it is, staring you right in the face.

You gather your wits. Carefully you explain that there is only one way to look at this. And that one way gives solidity. You argue that solidity is what makes it so that we can rectify all the various ways in which we each of us perceive the truth. But wait! That's just my perceived truth. It doesn't make any sense.

You get mad. You blurt out, "I don't care what you think." And you feel self righteous. Now, feeling good about yourself, you have nothing to prove. You don't need to be defensive. You soften. So now you're thinking, O.K., man. I'm open. Explain that to me again. Omigod! I care about what you think because I feel good about myself because I didn't care about what you think. It's a trap! That tricky Paradox has struck, wrapping its evil tentacles of irony around your truth.

You can't take it anymore. It's time to bail. You decide to let it go; to go with the flow and not be assertive or make any decisions. But! But! How can you decide to not decide? There's no way out. It's maddening. Besides, you are wondering if you have the energy to let go. No! No! How can it take energy to let go?

That's all you can take. You go screaming into the night, with the Paradox in close pursuit. Finally, exhausted, you give up. You yield to the Paradox. You let it take you completely. You've lost yourself. Nothing to prove. Nothing to maintain. What a load off of your mind. You begin to relax. Now you feel better. You feel good. You've lost your ego. You feel at peace with yourself. You haven't felt this good in a long time. You haven't felt this good being yourself in a long time. Self? You ask yourself, "How did I get to myself by giving myself up?". Yes, the Paradox has you now. But it's not to be dreaded. It's…. it's…. it's actually a benevolent creature.

You feel content in the moment, as you look confidently to the future. You now know that when you encounter a Paradox that you've found a truth that leads to a bigger truth and you are on the right path.

Segue

The Segue is a fearsome beast. It lives in the human mind. Its assault can be triggered by a sight, a sound, or a smell. But more often and more insidiously it is summoned... by a mere word. Which is why it is so dangerous.

Side tracked again - suddenly I'm speaking of and thinking about witches. We and all subjects come under its spell. (Witch's spell?)

Somewhere, (or so I've heard) there is a Segue-free zone. A zone, a place, where free unfettered thought is possible. A place where creativity flourishes. A place where the mechanics of the physical and the spiritual world can be accessed. Giving us - no - allowing us to act with genius and to be with peace of mind. Perhaps madness helps.

And it makes me mad. Damn it! The Segue has struck. And that's just what it's done. It's dammed my creative flow. I must struggle and fight my way back to the surface. Free myself from this water metaphor.

Maybe I've been too harsh. Maybe there are benevolent Segues. Or am I just under its spell - giving in.

A Segue-free zone. Hah! I am a dreamer.

Dreams! Yes, dreams! That's it.

Maybe there are benevolent Segues. This one, just now, having led me to dreamland. Dreams are perhaps the most Segue driven reality of all. But is it insidious or the ultimate insight? Being driven by subconscious Segues?

The ultimate potential of dreams is to free us from a life of being pitifully compelled to thought and action, by our pasts. And from accepting standards that mean nothing and that allow our lives to be squelched.

Dreams - the ultimate Paradox. Segue driven but paradoxically liberating us from that which keeps us bogged down. Perhaps the Paradox has been offered to us and exists to fight the malevolent Segue. The Segue has a huge thumb under which.....

Shit! Witches again! Dammit! I'm being sucked under! Now in the water metaphor again!

No! I'm better than that.

The Segue has a huge thumb under which it can keep our lives down if we let it. Refuse to allow it sovereignty over our souls and lives.

Summon the muse.
Carpe diem!
Seize the day!
Live without pre-determined priorities.
Seek the Segue-free zone.
No - don't seek it.
Be it!

Cast aside trying to achieve goals using strictly linear action, like a train pulled by an engine with a Segue wearing a striped cap, chuckling as it leads you along predetermined tracks.

Fly a kite.
Jump in a lake.
Look the other way.
Do something for no good reason.
Outsmart the Segue by acting dumb.
Outrun the Segue by standing stone still.

Don't fight it.
Surprise it by allowing it to come in your dreams.
Wash away the past in a huge cathartic rain of history.
Enter the Segue-free zone like a newborn.

And when you've done that, please come and find me.
And help me find my way.

Innuendo

The Innuendo is a devilish critter to behold. In any encounter, you'd like to know exactly what's going on. Tell it like it is. Give it to me straight.

But no, the Innuendo will slay you every time. Give you a pat on the back, tell you everything is alright, then torture you with an implication. You think you've been insulted, but you're not sure.

About to walk away, you figure you can take it, but the Innuendo will wield its implication with the skill of a master swordsman. Thrusting with wit and fending off your inquiry with its shield of vagueness.

You try and pin it down but it's as slippery as a greased pig. You demand clarity and directness. This only aggravates the fearsome Innuendo to call on its partner, Insinuation.

Before you know it, the truth is far out of reach; you feel like you're watching the evening news.

Driving you nuts, like ants in you pants, you feel like you've been had, even as Innuendo and Insinuation smile as if they like you. Careful! They'll try and get your trust.

Careful, man.

Just when you begin to think they didn't mean any more than they outright said, Innuendos and Insinuations are coming at you from all sides.

And still they smile.

An Offer From A Friend

I am an inventor, I guess you could say; my work primarily consisting of creating various phenomenon. (And you thought God did all that.) I have been hard at work down below.... ah.... er.... in my basement la-bore-atory.

A distant relative of mine (far distant) became well known for creating "Conflict."

He had hoped to become famous with this new concept and was quite surprised when he actually became infamous. The public outcry was deafening since previous to that time any outcry was unheard of.

Considering how quickly Conflict caught on, I suspect that the outcry was really a facade, a response shown outwardly to maintain the veneer of decency while inside a majority of people secretly enjoyed Conflict. It inflamed passions and did it with so much more ease than other ways that required dealing with the complexities of human nature and the dynamics of social existence and the human condition.

In time, as Conflict caught on, infamy seemed to be fame just the same.

Since then there have been some new developments by various do-gooders who hoped to gain some sort of notoriety themselves (Or so I assume. Why else would they take the effort?) by creating such things as "Compromise" and "Solutions".

The problem with Compromise and Solutions is that you can only sell them once for each Conflict.

I believe that my recent creation will be one that will be revered and put to use in many social situations and in the world of politics. I believe that my creation will be adopted around the world in a flash and I will never know want again.

I am in the final stages of creating the "Impasse".

The Impasse should effectively short circuit Compromise and Solution. I have carefully crafted it to be put to use in any Conflict or dilemma and to play on personal pride. It will cleverly make individuals and social groups identify themselves with certain concepts and ideologies that will inflame egos and once again give them those oh so simply employed channels to passion and feelings of being fully alive.

Politicians will love the Impasse, being able to ride the crest of a single Impasse for great lengths of time. The profits and kickbacks from politicians alone could well feed me, I hope, for eternity.

Like any good product a slogan will be helpful.

Words and communication have been the bread and butter of those seeking to effectively make use of Compromise and Solution, so a good marketing slogan for Impasse must co-opt and corrupt those words. Here it is: "Styx and stones can break my bones, but words can never thwart me."

Yes, I believe that Impasse can yield me many a soul.

And finally the coup de grâce is that once I have given the world Impasse I will distribute (using many different pen names) a plethora of instruction manuals for Compromise and Solution that on the surface appear to be legitimate guides and how-to manuals written to help understand the complexities of life and to empower people, but will, in fact, boggle people's minds with rules and regulations and arbitrary standards so that they will revert to the easy access of passion through simpler means.

A famous wise man once said, "everything should be made as simple as possible, but not simpler". These manuals will (without ever outwardly endorsing it) drive people to use methods such as denial and avoidance (ignore-ance) to achieve Compromise and Solution, but will in fact fall in the category of "simpler" – too simple.

Thus bringing them directly to an Impasse. Sheer genius, if I do say so myself.

Please allow me to introduce myself...

B. Elzebub

Space Flight

I ascended and as I rose I felt lighter and freer than I have ever felt before. Surely this was one astral trip to write home about. A thought crossed my mind. But it escaped unmolested by my practical mind. I began to attempt to ask myself questions. But before I could pose a question the answers came rendering the asking pointless. Being just as pointless, I let the answers go. My thoughts were like an M.C. Escher drawing; a labyrinth with no way out but not a trap. Rather a puzzle that was all things and there was no "out".

There was, however, direction. And it was clear that all roads lead home. Full circle. Except it was no circle. More of a rollercoaster. After a lifetime sojourn, arriving home again, leaner and stronger. I could see that the home was paradoxically a place of nurturing and sanctuary and at the same time it was only a gilded, orange grove scented, puffy cloud pillowed revolving door. Only the road and the dawn, the sun, the wind, and the rain, and the watch fire under stars, and sleep, and the road again.

I wanted to look back and look at that road I had been on. I wanted to gaze upon the earth, my home away from home for the better part of my last lifetime. I looked down upon her hoping for a glimpse of my path revealed to me. That was not to be. I realized that I was out of time. No, not out of time like the clock had run out. Out of time like there was no time. And as I looked down, there she was. The history of the earth unfolding – nay, not unfolding, but happening all at once right before my eyes. I could see the druids riding the dinosaurs. I could see great floods engulfing a plague of locusts. And there, there were volcanoes spewing out stone circles, great and small, with all their power condensed.

And the stone circle portals melted away revealing me ascending and rising, lighter and freer than I had ever felt before.

Tick Tock

(or how Alice discovered that Oz was really in Kansas)
(and how Brigadoon might emerge from the mist forever)

You can remove the tock from the clock,
but the clock would still tick.
Or, you can remove instead the tick from the clock,
but the clock would still tock.

But, perhaps, just maybe, if it were possible,
to remove both tock and tick,
then time would stand still as a stock,
and there would be no time to fix the clock.

But another theory has it that if you remove,
both tock and tick from the clock,
we would be free as a fool,
to do everything all at once. Cool.

Life would be free of restriction, constriction and friction,
and finally, at last, we'd be liberated from time,
to do anything as we please,
in any season without reason or rhyme.

What's more, is that this might free us,
from a lot of past pain and then,
with all the time in the world to do with as we please,
we could put Humpty Dumpty back together again.

Now that seems fine and dandy,
but there are many top theorists,
(they being me) who insist, you see,
that it might not be quite so handy.

Heading Out

It may be that while we talk and at once sing,
play and at the same time work,
and as we both walk and ride,
that everything would collide.

It may be that it's really not space, but time,
and not the tape measure but the chronometer,
that keeps all things apart,
keeping the horse ahead of the cart.

And it's time which allows us to breathe,
out and in, each exhalation and inhalation,
freeing our creativity in emptiness and fullness,
so that every expiration may be followed by an inspiration.

Now, I understand that the walrus and the carpenter,
are, as we speak, attempting to remove,
both the tick and the tock,
and if they succeed, we can throw away the clock.

Will we be free at last to live as we please,
unfettered by time, blessed with a free ride?
Or will all rush together with dire consequences,
as "once upon a time" and "happily ever after" collide?

Now, there is another consideration.
If the tock is removed,
leaving only the tick in the clock,
what is to be done with the now removed tock?

The preservation of energy theory says,
that to maintain the equilibrium,
there would be another clock,
somewhere else, that would only tock.

And would the clocks, one only ticking
    and one only tocking,
leave us oscillating from one moment to the next,
    and then,
from that next moment back to this one,
    nothing ever new to lose or gain,
trapped in a Groundhog Day, perhaps of pleasure,
    of indifference, or pain.

It seems to me that that we should take care,
should the walrus and the carpenter succeed,
to enjoy the feast before us as we live and breathe,
and have some fun and make sure, as we proceed...

To find a beautiful rhythm and rhyme,
should we be freed with them for all time.
And seek out sweet rides,
should they become our swan songs as all collides.

And to seek pleasure from one moment to the next,
should the next moment and this one,
be all we will ever again see,
becoming our final destiny.

    Goo goo, goo-joob.

Stay Hungry

Hypnotized Masses
Wearing Rose Colored Glasses
Never seeing things as they are
Fractured Child
Growing Up Wild
Stuck on earth but reaching for a star
Flame on, Rage on
Love everyone
Question everything solid.
Why life, why strife?
No longer do the basics sustain.
Hungry
Find out all you can,
More life in a pond
Than in the city
      (such a pity)
Turn me into a frog
And I'll bask on a log,
Leave me human.
O.K.
I'll learn to Adapt.
But time changes everything.
By the time I get to Phoenix
The Gryphon will be invisible.
      (not gone – invisible)
Learn To See
Fractured Child
The fissure allows access.

Don't ever get it all together.
You'll sink like a stone.
To touch a star
You must expand.
      (you can, you know)
Allow the matrix
Ungravity. Higher Laws.
Yo, Hypnotized Masses
Crush your glasses
Set sail and Just Let Go.
Play
Make a career of it
Invest in free time.
Stockpile freedom.
Touch
Revel in skin.
The mother of all grails.
Never forget.
Music
Sanctify It.
Take it to its Highest Form.
Most sublime...... Rock On!
Why then Hard Times?
Why then stupid Rhymes?
Muddle through the structure
And free the dance.
Hush-hush you say?
Never!!

Begone, my milquetoast friend.
I do love you
But you gotta go.
Come back when you're confused.
Too radical?
Born that way.
Find Me!
Through Fissures in Time and Space
Bodies require space.
Yeah, I know.
Resigned
To Hell with it
Redesign.
Yeah, redesign.
The stability of change.
Skinplay
Touchingmusic
Fractured Child, Hungry and Wild
Just let go.
Radical.
Dance any way you can.
That's all There Is.

Celestial Cex

Lunar excesses
Crash your love making.
It was easier
Before you became shy –
More aware.
Try it again –
And this time, breathe.
You may even laugh,
If you like.
Learn to pay attention –
Without your mind.
Feel the tide inside.
Surf's Up!
Catch that wave
And ride it home.
It's your wave
And yours alone.
Remember though
There's someone else
Whose life you're touching,
Riding a sister wave.
Now forget it again.
Love, fitting like a glove.
At first you feel it -
The enveloping warmth.
But now it's so natural.

Skin - Hot and Wet
Enter the pipeline
Be the wave.
Which one are you?
You are Neptune
You are Venus
Skin gives way to pure energy -
Skin's highest state,
Now porous.....
Goddess and God
Which sex are you?
Does it matter?
Keep breathing.
Sun and Moon
Surfer and Pipeline
Falling, yet not.
The sea creates its own gravity.
Breathe!
Breathe!!
Aaahhhhaaahhh
Laugh!
Out loud!!
Cry out!!!
Surfer emerges
From the pipeline.
The wave subsides,
The shore approaches.

You allow yourself
To be carried along.
As the sea subsides
Waves within you continue to come.
You're super sensitized now,
You feel every ripple
You soften.... shhhh....
As you are deposited on the shore.
Hallelujah!
You're not alone.
You're safe, loved.
Now you know which sex you are.
But it doesn't matter.
Your skin is once again your own.
You know because
Someone else is stroking it.
You understand now.
You understand not in your head
But in your heart.
There are no lunar excesses.
The heat of the Sun.
The pull of the Moon.
And Mother Earth
Who held her arms open
Welcoming you to her shores
Holds you now.
       You've been reborn.
       You've Made Love.

Earlier Excursions
(From The Way Back)

Adrienne

I was almost killed last week
Twice
With the same woman
It was a full Moon
Aries
People were ejaculating their steel-on-rubber bullets
Into the night
Impregnating pain in the hole they had no Love to fill
Her Neptune is low and square her Sun
I did nothing as the squealing projectile's pain
Challenged my fate
I knew (did I?) it was o.k.
She laughed - said she enjoyed it
She doesn't like to be touched.

Sleep

Oh sleep, to be free from alive,
Peace, to quench the thirst for nothing,
To blow free; dreams, solid, or both,
Reawakening, new, more alive, ready, steady again.

In Your Arms Fantasy

I'd give anything to hold;
To be held in your;
You in my, arms
right now!

Vibrating Independently?

The snow falls evenly
The fire crackles erratically
I might as well be at the ocean
for all of natures rhythms.
So comfortable
To be a part of those rhythms
And to vibrate independently –
Sort of.

Leather, Feathers, and Crystal

(Upon hearing of a friend's wedding
from a mutual juggler friend.)

I've had the news
About you twos
Juggled to me
By a friend of we
He said it was soon
I forget which moon
So here are some feathers,
Leather, and crystal
Our Love is true whether
You're near or distal.

Row, Row, Row Your Dream

Row, row, row your dream
Gently down the stream.
Merrily, merrily, merrily,
Life is but a boat.

Windfalls

direct and shape all thought to what you want
never question your motives
laugh at doubts as you let them slip on by.

laugh with and thrive on fortune and luck
build an arrogant confidence
with loving, laughing freeman spirit.

win in a staring contest with a stumbling block
till it backs down and reveals itself
to be nothing more than an event.

the causal link that binds the events
in what you so selfishly call your life
is your desires.

bridge that chasm, knowing
an ethereal thread sustains itself
windfalls only appear serendipitous.

Ankle Twist

Loosen up a bit and off for a run.
New shoes feel great.
An easy run to campground.
Body all feels fine.
Until.
With insane confidence.
Try to run down cliff.
Terror.
Ground rushes up.
Body too far forward.
Out of control.
Dark, can't see.
Can't plan landing.
Right foot hard to ground.
Knee bends, moment of relief.
Left foot down.
Ankle buckles.
Left leg kicks out.
Injury.
Shake it off a bit, swear.
Infuriated at self.
Walk comfortably but gingerly.
Woods path back.
Anticipate laid up.
Feel sort of good.
A little bit high.

This is the stuff of life.

Sandwiches are Square

What do you eat when there is nothing? It's clear as proverbial chrystal. Nothing. But you'd better start looking because as far as I know, without it you'll die. (without me!) I'll start looking as soon as I'm done etching or typing, if you will, a few notes with regards to the benefit of somebody, I hope.

Now. We are looking for food. I'll begin my search here. If I don't gain anything from my efforts in this region, I shall then expand my search to There. If, failing again to find sustenance is the case then I would move on to another There.

In this manner Heres become Theres and Theres become Heres. Very interesting. The identity of both are in jeopardy.

You know; it's crazy. Here I am hungry looking for food and I'm concerned about a dumb identity crisis. But not so dumb. If a Here could be a There, I could be a You. Don't laugh. I laughed at first but this thing is real.

Well, when you're hungry, you can't go worrying about your identity for very long so I took a philosophical outlook at the whole thing. Everything is transient in some sense. We (us people and animals and all the non-living objects) are all in the same boat.

In fact, identities themselves are transient. Son of a gun.

I'm an optimist. Thinking right away that rock I see is a peanut butter and jelly sandwich. Why not? We've got transient identities. But, not quite believing, I decided not to take a bite right out of it. I poke it with a stick. Sure enough - a rock.

Hungry, wondering what the hell is going on.

I've been to several Theres and one Here more than that. There I am. I've always wanted to say that but you can't. You just can't. It can't be.

I once read that when you're really hungry your mind wanders. Well, my mind always wanders. At least it seems to. I thought everybody had a mind born to roam. Well I read on and I learn to understand that the author of this book also thinks you should cage your mind. To, in effect, tie it down. He didn't say that in so many words but he didn't fool anybody. The guy was a square. (sandwiches are square)

Stay Cool

Music. Interrupted by a head trip.
Stop it and feel. The texture.
Get the flow but don't go.
Let it come to you.
First a rush. Then mellow.
Relax.
Write smoothly. Feel cool.
Be your tools. Pieces of art.
Until the rage subsides and love returns.
Try it. It works.
Relax. Stay cool.

Sarah Reflects On Roger

(written by Sarah of me)

Early morning - low mist, and the neighbors birds are carrying on as usual. Roger and I biked down to petersins for some last minute tripe. It will be a while before I see his back rising like a lighthouse over his khaki casted flanks. I remember the last time I left behind his behind in the tacoma terminal. Um. His shoulders give me faith in the strength of individuals and in man's ability to keep his LOVE alive.

A Few Poems Still In The Mill

Flat Flip Flies Straight

In Case Of Flood, Seek Higher Ground

Pitch Perfect Silence

Rainglades And Everforests

Sometimes it's so together
Like the wind breathing the weather

About the Author

I was born in Seattle and spent the first 30 years of my life in the Pacific Northwest. Well, except for 4 school years in a private Quaker boarding school in Pennsylvania, which was a great communal living experience. I think this had a far reaching and profound effect on my life. I have since lived in many different places, mostly favoring the West Coast; Olympia, Bellingham, San Juan Island, San Luis Obispo, Santa Cruz, Santa Fe, Maui, Kauai and currently Sebastopol, California. Integral in my experience has been a number of trips to Europe, mostly spending my time in the area around Innsbruck, Austria, which is my second home and where I have so many dear friends.

Work has also been varied; most of it being for myself. I have worked as a carpenter and with a partner built 2 houses in the mountains (one in Idaho, one in Washington) using (almost) exclusively hand tools. In Santa Cruz, I started my own business building and selling portable massage tables of my own design and did that for many years.

I love music; my favorites being classical music of the more sublime nature (Debussy, for one) and psychedelic era rock of which I consider the Beatles to be the ultimate. My favorite instrument is the human voice. Music has been a cornerstone of my life and has carried me through many peaceful and turbulent times.

I love to get out and ramble around on my mountain bike. It keeps me young; not the exercise so much as the playfulness and freedom of it.

And my most recent passion is playing strategic eurogame board games with friends.

Other Books by Roger Golden Brown

The Truth Seeker's Handbook has been published in print and as an eBook. I kept journals for over 20 years, writing almost every day. Much of the philosophy, the struggles leading to learning and the attitudes that helped me get through life appears in this book. It has a section dealing with major life themes, one about our relationship to the Earth, one retelling stories of serendipity, and finally a section of reminders to help along the way.

Two of those sections are available as their own books:

Themes of my Life
Reminders From Life for Life

Excerpt from The Truth Seeker's Handbook:

Delight in truth at all costs. We really must accept everything we experience. Simply say, yes, this is happening to me. We tend to avoid and repress and choose against less pleasant feelings. What a rip-off! They offer powerful information as to what is going on; information as to the reason why we don't at the moment have pleasant feelings. The desirable feelings validate flow and rightness. The unpleasant ones are the ones needing the most attention.

- - -

Insights has been published in print and as an eBook. This is a compilation of most of the journal entries which didn't appear in any of my other books, but that I felt needed to see the light of day. I organized them into such categories as Cosmic, Philosophy and Attitude, Love, Society, and several more.

Excerpt from Insights:

I heard Earth Angel on the radio today and thought about the American Dream and its surfacing in the 50's and the dreamy songs reflecting it. I was overwhelmed with a rush of rightness. Sure it is distorted. Sure its means are destructive. But the dream - to have comfort and ease and the time and space to relax and expand, time to create, to have comfortable homes is fine. It sparked a spiritual movement which unfortunately was complicated by an awesome opportunity to be corrupted by material and sensory numbing diversions. But the dream itself, it's not only the American Dream but a soul's dream. To mellow a life in a body. To find harmony. I'm all for it.

- - -

Heading Out is poetry and prose and has been published in print and as an eBook. Cryptic and cosmic might be good words to describe these writings; word adventures. Poetry is an individual thing and I can't say for sure you will like them, but look for it and check out the free eBook sample.

A short poem from Heading Out:

Popsicle process brings freedom ... in heat.
What was ice yields a watery treat.
When we allow ourselves to have what we need
That water fertilizes and brings life to our seed.

- - -

Encounters has been published in print and as an eBook. It is about encounters with women in my life that were romantic and sometimes intimate but does not include the girlfriends or lovers of duration. It is all journal entries in real time; usually my initial feelings, the encounter evolving, and finally myself seeking resolution and completion for myself and hopefully us. These encounters took place mostly during my 20's and 30's and are very gutsy and emotional. I have been a very emotional person and it may surprise some people to read a man's feelings essentially unedited.

Excerpt from Encounters:

> I approached her during a thunderstorm downpour on the main sunning deck (at Harbin Hot Springs). I was attracted to her and felt an immediate thrill from and affection for her. I wanted her. I spent some time with her and got to know her a little. I slept next to her on the sleeping deck. She let me know she needed space. She removed my hand gently from her body, but didn't let go. She held my hand a few moments more. What a beautiful softening of the space between us that she required. I was hurt and felt rejected, although I appreciated her communication and integrity. I cried. Strange sleep. Dreams. I felt again defeated but fought it, hung in there.

- - -

33 Years of Dreams has been published in print and as an eBook. Over a period of 33 years I wrote down a ton of dreams. A friend once said to me, why would anybody want to read anyone else's dreams? That got me to thinking but it came to me you could also ask why would anybody want to read anyone else's poetry? They are the same, in a way; kind of cryptic non-linear stories that take images and create something to be interpreted. After trimming out some of the uninteresting and poorly transcribed dreams it is, in its final form, almost 700 pages and is published in 2 volumes. They are for sale individually.

A dream from 33 Years of Dreams:

> I was with a pet, female, smiling Buffalo and a group of friends hanging out in the country. And with an alien friend who materialized to be with us. There was a river scene, after going through a gate. Rednecks were hassling us, then we saw three of our women being physically abused down the road a ways, by three men. We headed down in force (with our alien and Buffalo) to deal with it.

Where to Buy the Books

To buy the books in print go to my Author Page:
http://books2read.com/rogergoldenbrown

Versions of these books in eBook format can all be found at Smashwords, as well as free sample downloads:
https://www.smashwords.com/profile/view/Rogue17

Check out my Smashwords author interview here:
https://www.smashwords.com/profile/view/Rogue17154

Money For Art

Buying this book, I'll tell you right now, is good for your
    health.

Though it may seem, on the surface, to compromise your
    wealth.

This book you can open, and read and reread, whatever
    you find.

You'll get a new meaning, with each day's new light, and
    that's good for your mind.

A penny saved, is a penny earned, so they've always told
    you.

But listen carefully, to what I say to you now, and you'll
    know it rings true.

Reading the words in this book, is like a walk in the woods,
    and good for your heart.

And spending those pennies, will free your soul, if spent to
    buy art.

Please contact me should you want to comment or ask about
anything. Also I would appreciate any feedback if any typos
are discovered.

wordsmith@goldengalaxies.net

Thanks for reading.

www.ingramcontent.com/pod-product-compliance
Lightning Source LLC
Chambersburg PA
CBHW031604040426
42452CB00006B/404